The Peyote Cult

By

Paul Radin

First published in 1925

Published by Left of Brain Books

Copyright © 2023 Left of Brain Books

ISBN 978-1-397-66984-1

First Edition

All rights reserved. No part of this publication may be reproduced, distributed, or transmitted in any form or by any means, including photocopying, recording, or other electronic or mechanical methods, without the prior written permission of the publisher, except in the case of brief quotations permitted by copyright law. Left of Brain Books is a division of Left Of Brain Onboarding Pty Ltd.

PUBLISHER'S PREFACE

About the Book

"Peyote has never been a drug for thrill seekers. The small, hard cactus is difficult to obtain. It tastes vile, ingestion normally leads to painful vomiting, and the effects are more subtle than other psychedelics.

The Native American Peyote ceremony emerged at the turn of the 20th century, like the Ghost Dance, at a time when Native American culture was under much stress. It blended Christian and traditional beliefs, and used Peyote as a sacrament. The Peyote ceremony spread from the Southwest into the Plains and other culture regions. Participants reported a spiritual cleansing, and experienced healing effects, which may be the result of powerful natural antibiotics in Peyote.

This is one of the first ethnographic accounts of the Peyote ceremony. Paul Radin wrote this monograph, mostly consisting of first-hand accounts, as part of his 1925 ethnography of the Winnebago tribe, who live in Wisconsin. The Peyote 'Cult' did not die out as Radin thought it might, but grew into the Native American Church, which is still going strong today. This group fought the US legal system to get an exemption to use the cactus, which is a controlled substance, in their ceremonies."

(Quote from sacred-texts.com)

About the Author

Paul Radin (1883 - 1959)

"Paul Radin (April 2, 1883 - February 21, 1959) was a widely-read American anthropologist of the early twentieth century. A student of Franz Boas at Columbia, the Lodz-born Radin counted Edward Sapir and Robert Lowie among his classmates. He began years of productive fieldwork among the Winnebago Indians (now properly the Ho-Chunk Nation) in 1908. His books are several, but his most enduring publication to date is The Trickster (1956), which includes essays by pioneering Greek-myth scholar Karl Kerenyi and psychoanalyst C.G. Jung.

Radin taught at a number of colleges and universities, including Kenyon College in 1947, 1949-52."

(Quote from wikipedia.org)

CONTENTS

PUBLISHER'S PREFACE
GENERAL DESCRIPTION 1
    JOHN RAVE'S ACCOUNT OF THE PEYOTE CULT AND OF HIS
    CONVERSION 7
    O.L.'S DESCRIPTION OF THE PEYOTE CULT 14
    J.B.'S ACCOUNT OF THE LEADER OF THE PEYOTE 19
    ALBERT HENSLEY'S ACCOUNT OF THE PEYOTE 21
    J.B.'S PEYOTE EXPERIENCES 27
    J.B.'S ACCOUNT OF HIS CONVERSION 45
    JESSE CLAY'S ACCOUNT OF THE ARAPAHO MANNER OF GIVING
    THE PEYOTE, CEREMONY WHICH HE INTRODUCED AMONG THE
    WINNEBAGO IN 1912 49
    DEVELOPMENT OF THE RITUALISTIC COMPLEX 56
    DISSEMINATION OF THE DOCTRINE 62
    WHAT THE CONVERTS INTRODUCED 64
    THE ATTITUDE OF THE CONSERVATIVES 68

GENERAL DESCRIPTION

OWING to the great importance of one of the modem cults found among the Winnebago, the so-called Mescal or Peyote, it will be discussed here in some detail. Not only is this cult of great prominence in the life of the modem Winnebago, but as its inception and progress can be followed out in considerable detail it is of great significance for the study of their religion.

The ceremony is generally held in a building called by the Peyote worshipers a church, although it frequently takes place in the open also. In the early days of its organization as many meetings as possible were held. In 1910 there was a tendency to restrict the number and to have them generally take place on Saturday night. In 1913, after the first enthusism of the new converts had died out, the author was informed that the meetings were rarely held more than once a week. Around Christmas and beginning with July a series of meetings was held, lasting from a week to 10 days, as a rule. The Christmas meetings were not prominent in 1910, but the July ones seem to have been held from the beginning. They represent, of course, merely a substitution for the older pagan ceremonies and games that were held about that time.

In the early days the ceremony was opened by a prayer from the founder, and this was followed by an introductory speech. Thereupon the leader sang a Peyote song, to the accompaniment of a drum. Then another speech was delivered, and when it was finished the drum and other regalia were passed to the man to the right. This man, in turn, delivered a speech and sang a song, and when he was finished, passed the regalia to the third man, who subsequently passed it to the fourth one. The fourth man, when he was finished, returned it to the leader. In this way the regalia passed from one person to another throughout the night. It not infrequently happens that one of these four gets tired and gives up his place temporarily to some other member of the cult. At intervals they stopped to eat or drink peyote. At about midnight the peyote, as a rule, begins to affect some people. These generally arise and deliver self-accusatory speeches, and make more or less formal confessions, after which they go around shaking hands with everyone and asking forgiveness.

a. PEYOTE LEADERS

b. BURIAL HUTS

In 1910 the cult already had a rather definite organization. There was, at every performance, one leader (pl. 54, a) and four principal participants. John Rave (pls. 5, b; 55, b), the Winnebago who introduced the peyote, was always the leader whenever he was present. On other occasions leadership devolved upon some older member. The four other principal participants changed from meeting to meeting, although there was a tendency to ask certain individuals whenever it was possible. The ritualistic unit, in short, is a very definite one, consisting of a number of speeches and songs and in the passing of the regalia from one to the other of the four participants.

a. OLIVER LAMERE

During the early hours of the evening, before the peyote has begun to have any appreciable effect, a number of apparently intrusive features are found. These, for the most part, consist of speeches by people in the audience and the reading and explanation of parts of the Bible. After the peyote has begun to have an appreciable effect, however, the ceremony consists exclusively of a repetition of the ritualistic unit and confessions.

There is an initiation consisting of a baptism, always performed by John Rave. It is of a very simple nature. Rave dips his fingers in a peyote infusion and then passes them over the forehead of the new member, muttering at the same time the following prayer:

b. JOHN RAVE

"God, his holiness."

This is what the Winnebago words mean, although some of the younger members who have been strongly permeated with Christian teachings translate the prayer into, "God, the Son, and the Holy Ghost."

Whenever the ceremony is performed in the open a fireplace in the shape of a horseshoe is made. At one end of this fireplace is placed a very small mound of earth, called by Rave "Mount Sinai," and in front of this a cross is traced in the earth. Upon the small earth mound are placed the two "chief" peyote, the Bible and the staff. The latter, called by Rave the shepherd's crook, is always covered with beadwork, and generally has a number of evenly cut tufts of deer hair on the end and at intervals along its length. The sacred peyote, known as huŋka (i.e., "chief") are exceptionally large and beautiful specimens. They are regarded by a number of people, certainly by Rave, with undisguised veneration.

In addition to the above, there is found a large eagle feather fan, a small drum, arid a peculiar small type of rattle. To my knowledge, this type was unknown among the Winnebago before its introduction by the peyote eaters.

JOHN RAVE'S ACCOUNT OF THE PEYOTE CULT AND OF HIS CONVERSION

During 1893-94 I was in Oklahoma with peyote eaters.

IN the middle of the night we were to eat peyote. We ate it and I also did. It was the middle of the night when I got frightened, for a live thing seemed to have entered me. "Why did I do it?" I thought to myself. I should not have done it, for right at the beginning I have harmed myself. Indeed, I should not have done it. I am sure it will injure me. The best thing will be for me to vomit it up. Well, now, I will try it. After a few attempts I gave up. I thought to myself, "Well, now you have done it. You have been going around trying everything and now you have done something that has harmed you. What is it? It seems to be alive and moving around in my stomach. If only some of my own people were here! That would have been better. Now no one will know what has happened to me. I have killed myself."

Just then the object was about to come out. It seemed almost out and I put out my hand to feel it, but then it went back again. "O, my, I should never have done it from the beginning. Never again will I do it. I am surely going to die."

As we continued it became day and we laughed. Before that I had been unable to laugh.

The following night we were to eat peyote again. I thought to myself, "Last night it almost harmed me." "Well, let us do it again," they said. "All right, I'll do it." So there we ate seven peyote apiece.

Suddenly I saw a big snake. I was very much frightened. Then another one came crawling over me. "My God! where are these coming from?" There at my back there seemed to be something. So I looked around and I saw a snake about to swallow me entirely. It had legs and arms and a long tail. The end of this tail was like a spear. "O, my God! I am surely going to die now," I thought. Then I looked again in another direction and I saw a man with horns and long claws and with a spear in his hand. He jumped for me and I threw myself on the ground. He missed me. Then I looked hack and this time he started back, but it seemed to me that he was directing his spear at me. Again I threw myself on the ground and he missed me. There seemed to be no possible escape for me. Then suddenly it occurred to me, "Perhaps it is this peyote that is doing this thing to me?" "Help me, O medicine, help me! It is you who are doing this and you are holy! It is not these frightful visions that are causing this. I should have known that you were doing it. Help me!" Then my suffering stopped. "As long as the earth shall last, that long will I make use of you, O medicine!"

This had lasted a night and a day. For a whole night I had not slept at all.

Then we breakfasted. Then I said, when we were through, "Let us eat peyote again to-night." That evening I ate eight peyote.

In the middle of the night I saw God. To God living up above, our Father, I prayed. "Have mercy upon me! Give me knowledge that I may not say and do evil things. To you, O God, I am trying to pray. Do thou, O Son of God, help me, too. This religion, let me know. Help me, O medicine, grandfather, help me! Let me know this religion!" Thus I spoke and sat very quiet. And then I beheld the morning star and it was good to look upon. The light was good to look upon. I had been frightened during the night but now I was happy. Now as the light appeared, it seemed to me that nothing would be invisible to me. I seemed to see everything clearly. Then I thought of my home and as I looked around, there I saw the house in which I lived far away among the Winnebago, quite close to me. There at the window I saw my children playing. Then I saw a man going to my house carrying a. jug of whisky. Then he gave them something to drink and the one that had brought the whisky got drunk and bothered my people. Finally he ran away. "So, that is what they are doing," I thought to myself. Then I beheld my wife come and stand outside of the door, wearing a red blanket. She was thinking of going to the flagpole and was wondering which road she should take. "If I take this road I am likely to meet some people, but if I take the other road, I am not likely to meet anyone."

Indeed, it is good. They are all well—my brother, my sister, my father, my mother. I felt very good indeed. O medicine, grandfather, most assuredly you are holy! All that is connected with you, that I would like to know and that I would like to understand. Help me! I give myself up to you entirely!

For three days and three nights I had been eating medicine, and for three days and three nights I had not slept. Throughout all the years that I had lived on earth, I now realized that I had never known anything holy. Now, for the first time, I knew it. Would that some of the Winnebagoes might also know it!

Many years ago I had been sick and it looked as if this illness were going to kill me. I tried all the Indian doctors and then I tried all of the white man's medicines, but they were of no avail. "I am doomed. I wonder whether I will be alive next year." Such were the thoughts that came to me. As soon as I ate the peyote, however, I got over my sickness. After that I was not sick again. My wife had suffered from the same disease, and I told her that if she ate this medicine it would surely cure her. But she was afraid, although she had never seen it before. She knew that I used it, but nevertheless she was afraid of it. Her sickness was getting worse and worse and one day I said to her, "You are sick. It is going to be very difficult, but try this medicine anyhow. It will ease you." Finally she ate it. I had told her to eat it and then to wash herself and comb her hair and she would get well, and now she is well. Then I painted her face and took my gourd and began singing very much. Then I stopped. "Indeed, you are right," she said, "for now I am well." From that day on to the present time she has been well. Now she is very happy.

Black Water-spirit at about that time was having a hemorrhage and I wanted him to eat the peyote. "Well, I am not going to live anyhow," he said. "Well, eat this medicine soon then and you will get cured." Consumptives never were cured before this and now for the first time one was cured. Black Water-spirit is living to-day and is very well.

There was a man named Walking-Priest and he was very fond of whisky; he chewed and he smoked and he gambled. He was very fond of women. He did everything that was bad. Then I gave him some of the peyote and he ate it and he gave up all the had things he was doing. He had had a very dangerous disease and had even had murder in his heart. But to-day he is living a good life. That is his desire.

Whoever has any bad thoughts, if he will eat this peyote he will abandon all his bad habits. It is a cure for everything bad.

To-day the Indians say that only God is holy. One of the Winnebagoes has told me, "Really, the life that I led was a very bad one. Never again will I do it. This medicine is good and I will always use it." John Harrison and Squeaking-Wings were prominent members of the medicine dance; they thought much of themselves as did all the members of the medicine dance. They knew everything connected with this medicine dance. Both of them were gamblers and were rich because they had won very much in gambling. Their parents had acquired great possessions by giving medicines to the people. They were rich and they believed that they had a right to be selfish with their possessions. Then they ate peyote and ever since that time they have been followers of this medicine. They were really very ill and now they have been cured of it. Now if there are any men that might be taken as examples of the peyote, it is these three. Even if a man were blind and only heard about them he would realize that if any medicine were good, it is this medicine. It is a cure for all evil. Before, I had thought that I knew something but I really knew nothing. It is only now that I have real knowledge. In my former life I was like one blind and deaf. My heart ached when I thought of what I had been doing. Never again will I do it. This medicine alone is holy and has made me good and has rid me of all evil. The one whom they call God has given me this. That I know positively. Let them all come here; men and women; let them bring with them all that they desire; let them bring with them their diseases. If they come here they will get well. This is all true; it is all true. Bring whatever desires you possess along with you and then come and eat or drink this medicine. This is life, the only life. Then you will learn something about yourself, so come. Even if you are not told anything about yourself, nevertheless you will learn something of yourself. Come with your disease, for this medicine will cure it. Whatever you have, come and eat this medicine and you will have true knowledge once and for all. Learn of this medicine yourself through actual experience.

If you just hear about it you are not likely to try it. If you desire real knowledge about it try it yourself, for then you will learn of things that you had never known before. In no other way will you ever be happy. I know that all sorts of excuses will run through your mind for not partaking of it, but if you wish to learn of something good, try this. Perhaps you will think to yourself that it will be too difficult and this will seem an excuse to you for not trying it. But why should you act thus a If you partake of it, even if you feel some uncertainty about its accomplishing all the good that has been said of it, I know that you will say to yourself, "Well, this life is good enough." After you have taken it for the first time, it will seem as if they are digging a grave for you, that you are about to die; and you will not want to take it again. "It is bad," you will think to yourself. You will believe that you are going to die and you will want to know what is going to happen to you. The coffin will be set before you and then you will see your body. If you wish to inquire further about where you are going then you will learn something you have not known. Two roads there are, one leading to a hole in the earth and the other extending up above. You will learn something that you had not known before. Of the two roads, one is dark and the other is light. You must choose one of these while you are alive and so must you decide whether you wish to continue in your evil ways or whether you will abandon them. These are the two roads. The Peyote people see them. They claim that only if you weep and repent will you be able to obtain knowledge. Do not, as I said before, listen to others talking about it, but try the medicine yourself. That is the only way to find out. No other medicine can accomplish what this has done. If, therefore, you make use of it, you will live. After they have eaten peyote people throw aside all the (evil) ceremonies that they were accustomed to perform before. Only by eating the peyote will you learn what is truly holy. That is what I am trying to learn myself.

It is now 23 years since I first ate peyote, and I am still doing it (1912). Before that my heart was filled with murderous thoughts. I wanted to kill my brother and my sister. It seemed to me that my heart would not feel good until I killed one of them. All my thoughts were fixed on the warpath. This is all I thought of. Now I know that it was because the evil spirit possessed me that I felt that way. I was suffering from a disease. I even desired to kill myself;

I did not care to live. That feeling, too, was caused by this evil spirit living within me. Then I ate this medicine and everything changed. The brother and sister I wanted to kill before I became attached to and I wanted them to live. The medicine had accomplished this.

O.L.'S DESCRIPTION OF THE PEYOTE CULT

JOHN Rave belongs to the Bear clan, the members of which had the functions of what might be called sergeants-at-arms. He and his ancestors used to be in charge of the manupetci (i.e., the sergeants-at-arms lodge), to which all malefactors would be brought for punishment.

Rave, although he belonged to this highly respected class of people, was a bad man. He roamed from place to place. He has participated in all the ceremonies of the Winnebago, the medicine dance alone excepted. He had been married many times. Up to 1901 he was a heavy drinker. In that year he went to Oklahoma and while there ate the peyote. He then returned to the Winnebago and tried to introduce it among them, but none with the exception of a few relatives would have anything to do with it. This did not in any way discourage him, however, and he continued using the peyote, now and then getting a few converts.

There was not very much religion connected with it in the beginning and the reason people drank it was on account of the peculiar effects it had upon them. Nevertheless these Peyote people preached good things and gradually lost all desire for intoxicating drinks or for participating in the old Winnebago ceremonies. Then Rave began to do away with the old Indian customs. About four or five years ago the membership in the Peyote religion began to increase, for many people now noticed that those connected with the Peyote cult were the only people in the tribe leading a Christian life.

At this time the Bible was introduced by a young man named Albert Hensley (pls. 8, d; 9, d). He, too, had been a bad person, although he had been educated at Carlisle. Like Rave, he was a heavy drinker and fond of wandering.

During the last few years our members have increased so fast that now almost half the tribe belong to our religion. We all make efforts to lead a Christian life and we are succeeding very well.

We use the New Testament, especially the Revelations.

Our meetings take place at any time. We gather together in the evening, and as soon as everything is in readiness the leader arises and offers a prayer called, "Turning themselves over to the care of the Trinity." Then all sit down and the leader makes the regular announcements. The peyote is then passed around, either in the dry condition or steeped. The leader thereupon starts the singing. These are some of the songs:

1. Ask God for life and he will give it to us.

2. God created us so pray to him.

3. To the home of Jesus we are going, so pray to him.

4. Come ye to the road of the Son of God; come ye to the road.

Then Albert Hensley calls upon 12 educated members to translate and interpret certain portions of the Bible for the nonreading members. He arranges with the leader to have the singing stop at certain places so that some of these young men can speak. When these are finished, other individuals are called upon to give testimony. Hensley always talks and so does Rave.

John Rave baptizes by dipping his hand in a diluted infusion of peyote and rubbing it across the forehead of a new member, saying, "I baptize thee in the name of God, the Son, and the Holy Ghost, which is called God's Holiness."

The peyote eaters wanted to get baptized and unite with the church in Winnebago, but the clergyman in charge would not permit them, so they went and did their own baptizing through their leader, John Rave, who, though he is not educated, is full of real intelligence and religion.

If a person who is truly repentant eats peyote for the first time, he does not suffer at all from its effects. But if an individual is bullheaded, does not believe in its virtue, he is likely to suffer a good deal. This I know from my own experience. After eating peyote I grasped the meaning of the Bible, which before had been meaningless to me.

If a person eats peyote and does not repent openly, he has a guilty conscience, which leaves him as soon as the public repentance has been made.

Old men and women who had been brought up to worship animals and all kinds of spirits have cast them all away and in many instances burned their idols, not because they were told to do so but because they felt that way.

Whenever at our meetings a person wishes to pray, he does so; when he wishes to cry, he does so. Indeed, we show no timidity about worshiping God in the right way. In the Bible one often reads of Christ casting out the devils and of the people shouting, etc. So does the peyote act on us in the beginning, although afterwards its effects abate.

If a peyote eater relapses into his old way of living, then the peyote causes him great suffering.

At first our meetings were started without any rule laid down by the Bible, but afterwards we found a very good reason for holding our meetings at night. We searched the Bible and asked many ministers for any evidence for Christ's ever having held any meetings in the daytime, but we could find nothing to that effect. We did, however, find evidence that he had been out all night in prayer. As it is our desire to follow as closely as we can in the footsteps of Christ, we hold our meetings at night. Then, too, when we pray we wish to get as far away as possible from earthly things, and the night is the best time, for then we are not likely to be bothered by anything.

We have made earnest efforts to become Christians since we began drinking and eating this peyote, but many people say sarcastically that we have drunk ourselves into Christianity, and that we are demented. I am a peyote eater, but I have never found a demented person among them. We claim that there is virtue in the peyote. To you who do not believe and desire to find out let me quote the fourth chapter of the First Epistle of St. John:

"Beloved, believe not every spirit, but try the spirits whether they are of God; because many false prophets are gone out into the world.

"Hereby know ye the spirit of God. Every spirit that confesseth that Jesus Christ is come in the flesh is of God."

We claim that you can not find out anything by standing off at a distance and only talking about it. We claim that some earthly things can have the virtue of God, for instance, the Bible, which is entirely made up of earthly material—the ink, the paper, the cover—yet it has survived the ages.

J.B.'S ACCOUNT OF THE LEADER OF THE PEYOTE [1]

(Pl. 3)

AMONG the Winnebago there is a man named Little-Red-Bird, and when he reached middle age he began to travel around the world and learn different Indian languages. He used to travel inland a good deal. Once he joined a circus and crossed the ocean. He felt so ill while crossing that he wanted to die. Suddenly a wind came up and he got very frightened. He did not know what to do. Then he prayed to Earthmaker. When he came to the other side of the ocean there he saw a big island and a big city (London), and in this last place they held their circus. The chief of that country (the king) he met there.

When he came back to his own people he told them that on the other side of the ocean the Thunderbirds did not thunder. All they did was to drizzle. There was no lightning either. As he crossed the ocean on his return it thundered and lightened.

When he came home he was very glad to see his relatives and he offered tobacco in thanksgiving.

Shortly after this he traveled again and came to a band of Indians who were eating peyote. It was his custom to try everything when he went visiting. He did not realize what he was doing when he ate this medicine, but he did it anyhow.

---

[1] The narrator was a very lukewarm follower.

After a while he began to think of his manner of life, and he felt that he was doing wrong. All the evil he had done he remembered. Then he prayed to God. Suddenly it occurred to him, "Perhaps I am the only one doing this." Then he looked around and watched the others, and he saw them praying in the same manner.

Not long after that he came home, taking with him some of this medicine. He knew it was holy. At home he offered tobacco to it and kept on eating it. Soon it cured him of a disease he had. He tried to induce some of the others to try it, but they refused. After a while a few tried it, and the peyote movement began to spread. All the old customs that they had been accustomed to observe they abandoned. They gave up the medicine dance and the ceremonies connected with the clans. For that reason, therefore; the conservative people hated them; their own brothers and sisters hated them, for they had abandoned what were considered holy ceremonies.

ALBERT HENSLEY'S ACCOUNT OF THE PEYOTE [1]

(Pls. 8, d; 9, d)

I am 37 years old. It was 37 years ago that my mother gave birth to me in an old-fashioned reed lodge. When I was a year old she died and my grandmother took care of me. I had come into the world a healthy child, but bad luck was apparently to pursue me, for when I was 7 years old my grandmother died. Then my father took care of me. At that time he began to be a had man; he was a drunkard and a horse thief. He would frequently get into trouble and run away, always taking me along with him, however. On one occasion we fled to Wisconsin, and there we stayed two years. We got along pretty well, and there my father married again. By his second wife he had three children.

After a while he got into trouble again, and misfortune followed misfortune. People were killing each other, and I was left alone. If at any time of my life I was in trouble it was then. I was never happy. Once I did not have anything to eat for four days. We had fled to the wilderness, and it was raining continually. The country was flooded with high water, and we sat on the top of a tree. It was impossible to sleep, for if we went to sleep we would fall off into the water, which was very deep. The shore was quite far away. As we were prominent people, we soon

---

[1] This account is of great importance, because Hensley introduced a large number of Christian elements into the ceremony, the principal one being the Bible.

heard that my father had been freed. We were very happy, and went back to our people.

At that time a young man named Young-Bear was starting for Nebraska, and he said that he would take me along. I was very happy. So in that manner I was brought to this country. Here I have had only happy days. When my father got married everyone disliked me. When I worked I was working for my father, and all the money I earned I had to give to him.

After a while I went to school, and although I liked it I ran away and then went to school at Carlisle. I wanted to lead a good life. At school I knew that they would take care of me and love me. I was very shy and lacked a strong character at that time. If a person told me to do anything I would always obey immediately. Everybody loved me. I stayed there six months. I was also taught Christianity there. When I came hack to my country the Episcopalian people told me that they wanted me to be diligent in religious matters and never to forsake the religion of the Son of God. I also desired to do that. I entered the church that we had in our country and I stayed with them six years.

At that time the Winnebago with whom I associated were heavy drinkers, and after a while they induced me to drink also. I became as wicked as they. I learned how to gamble and I worked for the devil all the time. I even taught the Winnebago how to be bad.

After a while they began eating peyote, and as I was in the habit of doing everything I saw, I thought I would do it, too. I asked them whether I could join, and they permitted me. At that time I had a position at the county commissioner's office. I ate the peyote and liked it very much. Then the authorities tried to stop the Indians from eating peyote, and I was supposed to see that the law was enforced. I continued eating peyote and enjoying it.

All the evil that was in me I forgot. From that time to the present my actions have been quite different from what they used to be. I am only working for what is good; not that I mean to say that I am good.

After that I married and now I have three children, and it would not have been right for me to continue in my wickedness. I resolved that thereafter I would behave as a grown-up man ought to behave. I resolved never to be idle again and to work so that I could supply my wife and children with food and necessities, that I would be ready to help them whenever they were in need. Here in my own country would I remain till I died. This (peyote) religion was good. All the evil is gone and hereafter I will choose my path carefully.

I know the story about the origin of the peyote. It is as follows:

Once in the south, an Indian belonging to the tribe called Mescallero Apache was roaming in the country called Mexico, and went hunting in the high hills and got lost. For three days he went without water and without food. He was about to die of thirst but he continued until he reached the foot of a certain hill, on top of which he could find shade under a tree that was growing there. There he desired to die. It was with the greatest difficulty that he reached the place and when he got there, he fell over on his back and lay thus, with his body stretched toward the south, his head pillowed against something. He extended his right arm to the west and his left arm to the east, and as he did this, he felt something cool touch his hands. "What is it?" he thought to himself. So he took the one that was close to his right hand and brought it to his mouth and ate it. There was water in it, although it also contained food. Then he took the one close to his left hand and brought it to his mouth and ate it. Then as he lay on the ground a holy spirit entered him and taking the spirit of the Indian carried it away to the regions above. There he saw a man who spoke to him. "I have caused you to go through all this suffering, for had I not done it, you would never have heard of the proper (religion). It was for that reason that I placed holiness in what you have eaten. My Father gave it to me and I was permitted to place it on the earth. I was also permitted to take it back again and give it to some other Indians.

"At present this religion exists in the south but now I wish to have it extended to the north. You Indians are now fighting one another, and it is for the purpose of stopping this, that you might shake hands and partake of food together, that I am giving you this peyote. Now you should love one another. Earthmaker is my father. Long ago I sent this gospel across the ocean but you did not know of it. Now I am going to teach you to understand it." Then he led him into a lodge where they were eating peyote. There he taught him the songs and all that belonged to this ceremony. Then he said to him, "Now go to your people and teach them all that I have told you. Go to your people in the north and teach them. I have placed my holiness in this that you eat. What my father gave me, that I have placed therein."

Then he told him to go home. He thought he had been dead, but it was really his spirit that had left him. After a while the man got well again.

There were many peyote near the place where he was lying and these he picked before he started. Then he went back to his lodge. He thought he had been lost, but it seemed hardly possible to him that this was the case. His being lost in the hills seemed to symbolize to him the condition of the people before they had eaten the peyote; they would be lost and then find their way again.

On his return he built a peyote lodge and for four nights he taught the people how to eat peyote. He did not, however, teach it as he was told, nor did he teach it thoroughly. These to whom he taught it used it for a purpose different from what it was intended. [1]They used it for war and for horse stealing. They, however, continued to eat the peyote, but they really ate too much of it. After a while the leader began thinking that the medicine might harm them, so he told them to hide it. The man did not know that even at that time a big war party was coming upon them. This tribe was almost destroyed.

They lost the peyote. One day, however, it was taught to a Comanche. He ate it and prayed to Earthmaker. Then it was taught to the Cheyenne and to the Arapaho and to the Caddo. The Tonkawa, the Apache, and the Mescallero Apache were the ones who had lost the medicine. When these other tribes began to eat this medicine they heard about it and they remembered that they also had long ago eaten it.

There was an old man in Oklahoma who knew the mescal country very well and he went down to old Mexico and stayed there for a year. When he returned he taught it to the Oto and the Oto taught it to us.

It is a true religion. The peyote is fulfilling the work of God and the Son of God. When the Son of God came to the earth he was poor, yet people spoke of him; he was abused. It is the same now with the peyote. The plant itself is not much of a growth, yet the people are talking about it a good deal; they are abusing it, they are trying to stop its use. When the Son of God came to earth the preachers of that time were called Pharisees and

---

[1] This is clearly Hensley's interpretation.

Scribes. They doubted what the Son of God said and claimed that he was an ordinary man. So it is to-day with the Christian Church; they are the Pharisees and Scribes, they are the doubters. They say that this is merely a plant, that it is the work of the devil. They are trying to stop its use and they are calling it an intoxicant, but this is a lie. If they will but come and see this ceremony they will realize this.

J.B.'S PEYOTE EXPERIENCES

WHEN my father and mother asked me to come to the Missouri River (Nebraska) I knew they had eaten peyote and I did not like it. I had been told that these peyote eaters were doing wrong, and therefore I disliked them; I had heard that they were doing everything that was wicked. For these reasons we did not like them. About this time they sent me money for my ticket, and since my brothers and sisters told me to go, I went. Just as I was about to start my youngest sister, the one to whom we always listened most attentively, said to me, "Older brother, do not you indulge in this medicine eating (peyote) of which so much is said." I promised. Then I started out.

As soon as I arrived (in Nebraska) I met some people who had not joined the peyote eaters and who said to me, "Your relatives are eating the peyote and they sent for you that you also might eat it. Your mother, your father, and your younger sister, they are all eating it." Thus they spoke to me. Then they told me of some of the bad things it was reported that these people had done. I felt ashamed and I wished I had not come in the first place. Then I said that I was going to eat the medicine.

After that I saw my father, mother, and sister. They were glad. Then we all went to where they were staying. My father and I walked (alone). Then he told me about the peyote eating. "It does not amount to anything, all this that they are doing, although they do stop drinking. It is also said that sick people get well. We were told about this and so we joined, and, sure enough, we are practically well, your mother as well as I. It is said that they offer prayers to Earthmaker (God)," he said. He kept on talking. "They are rather foolish. They cry when they feel very happy about anything. They throw away all of the medicines that they possess and know. They give up all the blessings they received while fasting and they give up all the spirits that blessed them in their fasts. They also stop smoking and chewing tobacco. They stop giving feasts, and they stop making offerings of tobacco. Indeed, they burn up their holy things. They burn up their war bundles. They are bad people. They give up the Medicine Dance. They burn up their medicine bags and even cut up their otter-skin bags. They say they are praying to Earthmaker (God) and they do so standing and crying. They claim that they hold nothing holy except Earthmaker (God). They claim that all the things that they are stopping are those of the bad spirit (the devil), and that the bad spirit (the devil) has deceived them; that there are no spirits who can bless; that there is no other spirit except Earthmaker (God)." Then I said, "Say, they certainly speak foolishly." I felt very angry toward them. "You will hear them, for they are going to have a meeting tonight. Their songs are very strange. They use a very small drum," said he. Then I felt a very strong desire to see them.

After a while we arrived. At night they had their ceremony. At first I sat outside and listened to them. I was rather fond of them. I stayed in that country and the young peyote eaters were exceedingly friendly to me. They would give me a little money now and then and they treated me with tender regard. They did everything that they thought would make me feel good, and in consequence I used to speak as though I liked their ceremony. However, I was only deceiving them. I only said it because they were so good to me. I thought they acted in this way because (the peyote) was deceiving them.

Soon after that my parents returned to Wisconsin, but when they left they said they would come back in a little while. So I was left there with my relatives, who were all peyote followers. For that reason they left me there. Whenever I went among the nonpeyote people I used to say all sorts of things about the peyote people, and when I returned to the peyote people I used to say all sorts of things about the others.

I had a friend who was a peyote man and he said to me, "My friend, I wish very much that you should eat the peyote." Thus he spoke and I answered him, "My friend, I will do it, but not until I get accustomed to the people of this country. Then I will do it. The only thing that worries me is the fact that they are making fun of you. And in addition, I am not quite used to them." I spoke dishonestly.

I was staying at the place where my sister lived. She had gone to Oklahoma; she was a peyote follower. After a while she returned. I was then living with a number of women. This was the second time (there) and from them I obtained some money. Once I got drunk there and was locked up for six days. After my sister returned she and the others paid more attention than ever to me. Especially was this true of my brother-in-law. They gave me horses and a vehicle. They really treated me very tenderly. I knew that they did all this because they wished me to eat the peyote. I, in my turn, was very kind to them. I thought that I was fooling them and they thought that they were converting me. I told them that I believed in the peyote because they were treating me so nicely.

After a while we moved to a certain place where they were to have a large peyote meeting. I knew they were doing this in order to get me to join. Then I said to my younger sister, "I would be quite willing to eat this peyote (ordinarily), but I don't like the woman with whom I am living just now and I think I will leave her. That is why I do not want to join now, for I understand that when married people eat medicine (peyote) they will always have to stay together. Therefore I will join when I am married to some woman permanently." Then my brother-in-law came and she told him what I had said, and he said to me, "You are right in what you say. The woman with whom you are staying is a married woman and you can not continue living with her. It is null and void (this marriage) and we know it. You had better join now. It will be the same as if you were single. We will pray for you as though you were single. After you have joined this ceremony, then you can marry any woman whom you have a right to marry (legally). So, do join tonight. It is best. For some time we have been desirous of your joining but we have not said anything to you. It is Earthmaker's (God's) blessing to you that you have been thinking of this," said he.

Therefore I sat inside the meeting place with them. One man acted as leader. We were to do whatever he ordered. The regalia were placed before him. I wanted to sit in some place on the side because I thought I might get to crying like the others. I felt ashamed of myself.

Then the leader arose and talked. He said that this was an affair of Earthmaker's (God's), and that he (the leader) could do nothing on his own initiative; that Earthmaker (God) was going to conduct the ceremony. Then he said that the medicine (peyote) was holy and that he would turn us all over to it; that he had turned himself over to it and wished now to turn all of us over to it. He said further, "I am a very pitiable (figure) in this ceremony, so when you pray to Earthmaker, pray also for me. Now let us all rise and pray to Earth-maker (God)." We all rose. Then he prayed. He prayed for the sick, and he prayed for those who did not yet know Earthmaker. He said that they were to be pitied. When he had finished we sat down. Then the peyote was passed around. They gave me five. My brother-in-law said to me, "If you speak to this medicine (peyote), it will give you whatever you ask of it. Then you must pray to Earthmaker, and then you must eat the medicine." However, I ate them (the peyote) immediately, for I did not know what to ask for and I did not know what to say in a prayer to Earthmaker (God). So I ate the peyote just as they were. They were very bitter and had a taste difficult to describe. I. wondered what would happen to me. After a while I was given five more and I also ate them. They tasted rather bitter. Now I was very quiet. The peyote rather weakened me. Then I listened very attentively to the singing. I liked it very much. I felt as though I were partly asleep. I felt different from (my normal self), but when I (looked around) and examined myself, I saw nothing wrong about myself. However, I felt different from (my normal self). Before this I used to dislike the songs. Now I liked the leader's singing very much. I liked to listen to him.

They were all sitting very quietly. They were doing nothing except singing. Each man sang four songs and then passed the regalia to the next one. (Each one) held a stick and an eagle's tail feather in one hand and a small gourd rattle, which they used to shake while singing, in the other. One of (those) present used to do the drumming. Thus objects would pass around until they came back to the leader, who would then sing four songs. When these were finished, he would place the various (things) on the ground, rise, and pray to Earthmaker (God) . Then he called upon one or two to speak. They said that Earthmaker (God) was good and that the peyote was good, and that whosoever ale this medicine (peyote) would be able to free himself from the bad spirit (the devil); for they said that Earthmaker forbids us to commit sins. When this was over they sang again.

After midnight, every once in a while (I heard) someone cry. In some cases they would go up to the leader and talk with him. He would stand up and pray with them. They told me what they were saying. They said that they were asking (people) to pray for them, as they were sorry for their sins and that they might be prevented from committing them again. That is what they were saying. They cried very loudly. I was rather frightened. (I noticed also) that when I closed my eyes and sat still, I began to see strange things. I did not get sleepy in the least. Thus the light (of morning) came upon me. In the morning, as the sun rose, they stopped. They all got up and prayed to Earthmaker (God) and then they stopped.

During the daytime I did not get sleepy in the least. My actions were a little different (from my usual ones). Then they said, "Tonight they are going to have another meeting. Let us go over. They say that is the best (thing) to do and thus you can learn it (the ceremony) right away. It is said that their spirits wander over all the earth and the heavens also. All this you will learn and see," they said. "At times they die and remain dead all night and all day. When in this condition they sometimes see Earthmaker (God), it is said." One would also be able to see where the bad spirit lived, it was said.

So we went there again. I doubted all this. I thought that what they were saying was untrue. However, I went along anyhow. When we got there, I had already eaten some peyote, for I had taken three during the day. Now near the peyote meeting an (Indian) feast was being given and I went there instead. When I reached the place, I saw a long lodge: The noise was terrific. They were beating an enormous drum. The sound almost raised me in the air, so (pleasurably) loud did it sound to me. Not so (pleasurable) had things appeared at those affairs (peyote meetings) that I had lately been attending. There I danced all night and I flirted with the women. About day I left and when I got back the peyote meeting was still going on. When I-got back they told me to sit down at a, certain place. They treated me very kindly. There I again ate peyote. I heard that they were going to have another meeting near by on the evening of the same day. We continued eating peyote the whole day at the place where we were staying. We were staying at the house of one of my relatives. Some of the boys there taught me a few songs. "Say, when you learn how to sing, you will be the best singer, for you are a good singer as it is. You have a good voice," they said to me. I thought so myself.

That night we went to the place where the peyote meeting was to take place. They gave me a place to sit and treated me very kindly. "Well, he has come," they even said when I got there, "make a place for him." I thought they regarded me as a great man. John Rave, the leader, was to conduct the (ceremony). I ate five peyote. Then my brother-in-law and my sister came and gave themselves up. They asked me to stand there with them. I did not like it, but I did it nevertheless. "Why should I give myself up? I am not in earnest, and I intend to stop this as soon as I get back to Wisconsin. I am only doing this because they have given me presents," I thought. "I might just as well get up, since it doesn't mean anything to me." So I stood up. The leader began to talk and I (suddenly) began to feel sick. It got worse and worse and finally I lost consciousness entirely. When I recovered, I was lying flat on my back. Those with whom I had been standing were still standing there. I had (as a matter of fact) regained consciousness as soon as I fell down. I felt like leaving the place that night, but I did not do it. I was quite tired out. "Why have I done this?" I said to myself. "I promised (my sister) that I would not do it." So I thought and then I tried to leave, but I could not. I suffered intensely. At last daylight came upon me. Now I thought that they regarded me as one who had a trance and found out something.

Then we went home and they showed me a passage in the Bible where it said that it was a shame for any man to wear long hair. That is what it said, they told me. I looked at the passage. I was not a man learned in books, but I wanted to give the impression that I knew how to read, so I told them to cut my hair, for I wore it long at that time. After my hair was cut I took out a lot of medicine that I happened to have in my pockets. Those were courting medicines. There were many small bundles of them. All these, together with my hair, I gave to my brother-in-law. Then I cried and my brother-in-law also cried. Then he thanked me. He told me that I understood and that I had done well. He told me that Earthmaker (God) alone was holy; that all the things (blessings and medicines) that I possessed were false; that I had been fooled by the bad spirit (devil). He told me that I had now freed myself from much of this (bad influence). My relatives expressed their thanks fervently.

On the fourth night they had another meeting and I went to it again. There I again ate (peyote). I enjoyed it and I sang along with them. I wanted to be able to sing immediately. Some young men were singing and I enjoyed it, so I prayed to Earthmaker, asking him to let me learn to sing right away. That was all I asked for. My brother-in-law was with me all the time. At that meeting all the things I had given my brother-in-law were burned up.

The fact that he (my brother-in-law) told me that I understood pleased me, and I felt good when daylight came. (As a matter of fact) I had not received any knowledge.

After that I would attend meetings every once in a while, and I looked around for a woman whom I might marry permanently. Before long that was the only thing I thought of when I attended the meetings.

On one occasion we were to have a meeting of men and I went to the meeting with a woman, with whom I thought of going around the next day. That was (the only) reason I went with her. When we arrived, the one who was to lead asked me to sit near him. There he placed me. He urged me to eat a lot of peyote, so I did. The leaders (of the ceremony) always place the regalia in front of themselves; they also had a peyote placed there. The leader placed a very small one in front of himself this time. "Why does he have a very small one there?" I thought to myself. I did not think much about it.

It was now late at night and I had eaten a lot of peyote and felt rather tired. I suffered considerably. After a while I looked at the peyote and there stood an eagle with outspread wings. It was as beautiful a sight as one could behold. Each of the feathers seemed to have a mark. The eagle stood looking at me. I looked around thinking that perhaps there was something the matter with my sight. Then I looked again and it was really there. I then looked in a different direction and it disappeared. Only the small peyote remained. I looked around at the other people but they all had their heads bowed and were singing. I was very much surprised.

Some time after this (I saw) a lion lying in the same place (where I had seen the eagle). I watched it very closely. It was alive and looking at me. I looked at it very closely, and when I turned my eyes Away just the least little bit it disappeared. "I suppose they all know this and I am just beginning to know of it," I thought. Then I saw a small person (at the same place). He wore blue clothes and a shining brimmed cap. He had on a soldier's uniform. He was sitting on the arm of the person who was drumming, and he looked at every one. He was a little man, perfect (in all proportions). Finally I lost sight of him. I was very much surprised indeed. I sat very quietly. "This is what it is," I thought, "this is what they all probably see and I am just beginning to find out."

Then I prayed to Earthmaker (God): "This, your ceremony, let me hereafter perform."

As I looked again, I saw a flag. I looked more carefully and (I saw) the house full of flags. They had the most beautiful marks on them. In the middle (of the room) there was a very large flag and it was a live one; it was moving. In the doorway there was another one not entirely visible. I had never seen anything so beautiful in all my life before.

Then again I prayed to Earthmaker (God). I bowed my head and closed my eyes and began (to speak). I said many things that I would ordinarily never have spoken about. As I prayed, I was aware of something above me and there he was; Earthmaker (God) to whom I was praying, he it was. That which is called the soul, that is it, that is what one calls Earthmaker (God). Now this is what I felt and saw. The one called Earthmaker (God) is a spirit and that is what I felt and saw. All of us sitting there, we had all together one spirit or soul; at least that is what I learned. I instantly became the spirit and I was their spirit or soul. Whatever they thought of, I (immediately) knew. I did not have to speak to them and get an answer to know what their thoughts had been. Then I thought of a certain place, far away, and immediately I was there; I was my thought.

I looked around and noticed how everything seemed about me, and when I opened my eyes I was myself in the body again. From this time on, I thought, thus I shall be. This is the way they are, and I am only beginning, to be that way. "All those that heed Earth-maker (God) must be thus," I thought. "I would not need any more food," I thought, "for was I not my spirit? Nor would I have any more use of my body," I felt. "My corporeal affairs are over," I felt.

Then they stopped and left, for it was just dawning. Then someone spoke to me. I did not answer, for I thought they were just fooling, and that they were all like myself, and that (therefore) it was unnecessary for me to talk to them. So when they spoke to me I only answered with a smile. "They are just saying this to me because (they realize) that I have just found out," I thought. That was why I did not answer. I did not speak to anyone until noon. Then I had to leave the house to perform one of nature's duties and someone followed me. It was my friend. He said, "My friend, what troubles you that makes you act as you do?" "Well, there's no need of your saying anything, for you know it beforehand," I said.

Then I immediately got over my trance and again got into my (normal) condition, so that he would have to speak to me before L knew his thoughts. I became like my former self. It became necessary for me to speak to him.

Then I spoke to him and said, "My friend, let us hitch up these horses and then I will go wherever you like, for you wish to speak to me and I also want to go around and talk to you." Thus I spoke to him. "If I were to tell you all that I have learned, I would never be able to stop at all, so much have I learned," I said to him. "However, I would enjoy telling some of it." "Good," said he. He liked it (what I told him) very much. "That is what I am anxious to hear," said he. Then we went after the horses. We caught one of them but we could not get the other. He got away from us and we could not find him. We hunted everywhere for the horse but could not discover where he had run to. Long afterwards we found it among the whites.

Now since that time (of my conversion) no matter where I am, I always think of this religion. I still remember it and I think I will remember it as long as I live. It is the only holy thing I have been aware of in all my life.

After that whenever I heard of a peyote meeting, I went to it. However, my thoughts were always fixed on women. "If I were married (legally) perhaps these thoughts will leave me," I thought. Whenever I went to a meeting now I tried to eat as many peyote as possible, for I was told that it was good to eat them. For that reason I ate them. As I sat there I would always pray to Earthmaker (God). Now these were my thoughts. If I were married, I thought as I sat there, I could then put all my thoughts on this ceremony. I sat with my eyes closed and was very quiet.

Suddenly I saw something. This was tied up. The rope with which this object was tied up was long. The object itself was running around and around (in a circle). There was a pathway there in which it ought to go, but it was tied up and unable to get there. The road was an excellent one. Along its edge bluegrass grew and on each side there grew many varieties of pretty flowers. Sweet-smelling flowers sprang up all along this road. Far off in the distance appeared a bright light. There a city was visible of a beauty indescribable by tongue. A cross was in full sight. The object that was tied up would always fall just short of reaching the road. It seemed to lack sufficient strength to break loose (of what was holding it). (Near it) lay something which would have given it sufficient strength to break its fastenings, if it were only able to get hold of it.

I looked at what was so inextricably tied up and I saw that it was myself. I was forever thinking of women. "This it is to which I am tied," I thought. "Were I married, I would have strength enough to break my fastening and be able to travel in the good road," I thought. Then daylight came upon us and we stopped.

Then I thought of a man I used to know who was an old peyote-man. He always spoke to me very kindly. I went over to see him. I thought I would tell him what had happened to me. When I arrived there he was quite delighted. It was about noon and he fed my horses and asked me to eat with him. Then when we were through eating, I told him what had happened to me. He was very glad and told me that I was speaking of a very good thing. Then (finally) he said, "Now I shall tell you what I think is a good thing (for you to do). You know that if an old horse is balky, you cannot break him of (this habit); even if you bought him and tried to break him (of this habit) you would not succeed. If, indeed, you succeeded it would only be after very hard work. However, if you had a very young horse, you could train it in any way you wished. So it is in everything. If you marry a woman who has been in the habit of marrying frequently, it would be difficult for her to break herself of a habit she loves. You are not the one she loves. If you marry her you will lead a hard life. If you wish to get married, take your time. There are plenty of good women. Many of them are at (government) schools and have never been married. I think you would do best if you waited for some of these before marrying. They will return in the middle of the summer. So, don't think of any of these women you see around here, but wait until then and pray to Earth-maker patiently. That would be the best, I think." I liked what he told me and thanked him. I decided to accept his advice, and I did not look around for women after that. I was to wait about three months and (during that time) I paid strict attention to the peyote ceremony.

On one occasion while at a meeting, I suffered (great pain). My eyes were sore and I was thinking of many things. "Now I do nothing but pay attention to this ceremony, for it is good." Then I called the leader over to me and said to him, "My elder brother, hereafter only Earthmaker (God) shall I regard as holy. I will make no more offerings of tobacco. I will not use any more tobacco. I will not smoke and I will not chew tobacco. I have no further interest in these. Earthmaker (God) alone do I desire (to serve). I will not take part in the Medicine Dance again. I give myself up (to you). I intend to give myself up to Earthmaker's (God's) cause." Thus I spoke to him. "It is good, younger brother," he said to me. Then he had me stand up and he prayed to Earthmaker (God). He asked Earthmaker (God) to forgive me my sins.

The next morning I was taken home. My eyes were sore and I could not see. They took me back to a house and there they put a solution of the peyote into my eyes and I got well in a week.

One night, when I was asleep, I dreamed that the world had come to an end. Some people Earthmaker (God) took, while some belonged to the bad spirit (the devil). I belonged to the bad spirit (the devil). Although I had given myself up (become a peyote-man), I had not as yet been baptized. That was why Earthmaker (God) did not take me. All those who belonged to Earthmaker (God) were marked, but I was not. I felt very bad about it when I woke up, although I had only dreamed about it. I felt very bad indeed. I wanted them to hurry and have another peyote meeting soon. I could hardly wait until I reached the place where the next meeting was to take place. I immediately told the leader (what I wanted) and asked him to baptize me and he baptized me in the morning. After that morning I felt better.

Then I went to work and I worked with a railroad work-gang. I was still working when the time for the midsummer celebration approached. I always went to the peyote meeting on Saturday nights.

The old man was right in what he had told me. The girl students returned in the summer. Shortly (after they returned) a man, a friend of mine who had gone around with me, asked me if I wanted to get married. "Yes, I do," I answered. Then he said, "Listen, I have been thinking of something. What kind of a woman do you wish to marry?" I told him what I had in mind. Then he said, "Come home with me. I have a younger sister. I want her to marry a good man; I would like to have her marry you," he said. Then I went home with him. When we got there (and discussed the matter) the girl gave her consent. The parents also consented.

So there I got married and what I expected has taken place and I have lived with her ever since. On one occasion, after she was used to me, she told me this. (Before she had married she had determined that) if she ever got married, she would not care to marry a very young man. "I wanted a man who ate peyote and who paid attention to the ceremony." Such a man she desired and such a man was I, she said. She loved me, she said, and she was glad that she had married me. This is what she had asked Earthmaker (God) in prayer. "And indeed it has happened as I wished," she said. She believed it was the will of Earthmaker (God) that we had done this, she said. She was therefore glad (that she had married me). Together we gave ourselves up (to the peyote) at a peyote meeting. From that time on we have remained members of the peyote (ceremony).

Many things are said under the influence of the peyote. The members (would) get into a kind of trance and speak of many things. On one occasion they had a peyote meeting which lasted two nights. I ate a good deal of peyote. The next morning I tried to sleep. I suffered a great deal. I lay down in a very comfortable position. After a while a (nameless) fear arose in me. I could not remain in that place, so I went out into the prairie, but here again I was seized with this fear. Finally I returned to a lodge near the lodge in which the peyote meeting was being held and lay down alone. I feared that I might do something foolish to myself (if I remained there alone), and I hoped that someone would come and talk to me. Then someone did come and talk to me, but I did not feel better, so I thought I would go inside where the meeting was going on. "I am going inside," I said to him. He laughed. "Alright, do so," said he. I went in and sat down. It was very hot and I felt as though I were going to die. I was very thirsty but I feared to ask for water. I thought that I was certainly going to die. I began to totter over.

I died, and my body was moved by another life. It began to move about; to move about and make signs. It was not I and I could not see it. At last it stood up. The regalia—eagle feathers and gourds—these were holy, they said. They also had a large book there (the Bible). These my body took and what is contained in that (book) my body saw. It was a Bible. The regalia were not holy, but they were good ornaments. My body told them that; and that if any person paid attention to Earthmaker's (God's) ceremony, he would be hearkening to what the Bible said; that, likewise, my body told them. Earthmaker's son (God's son) said that he was the only way. This means that one can only get life from the Word. (My) body spoke of many things and it spoke of what was true. Indeed it spoke of many things. It spoke of all the things that were being done (by the pagan Indians) and which were evil. A long time it spoke. At last it stopped. Not I, but my body standing there, had done the talking. Earthmaker (God) had done his own talking. I would be confessing myself a fool if I were to think that I had said all this, it (my body) told me.

After a while I returned to my normal human condition. Some of those there had been frightened, thinking that I had gone crazy. Others had liked it. It was discussed a good deal. They called it the "shaking" state. It was said that the condition in which I was, was not part of Earthmaker's (God's) religion. I was told that whoever ate a lot of peyote would, through the peyote, be taught the teachings of Earthmaker (God). Earthmaker's (God's) ways and man's ways were different. Whoever, therefore, wished to help this religion must give himself up (to it). If you ate a good deal of this peyote and believed that it could teach you something, then it assuredly would do so. That, at least, is the way in which I understand the matter.

Once we had a meeting at the home of a member who was sick. The sick would always get well when a meeting was held in their home, and that is why we did it. At that meeting I got into the "shaking" condition again. My body told (us) how our religion (peyote) was an affair of Earthmaker's (God's) and even if one knew only a portion of it, one could still see (partake of) Earthmaker's (God's) religion.

Thus it went on talking. "Earthmaker (God), His Son (Christ) and His Holiness (the Holy Ghost), these are the three ways of saying it. Even if you know one (of these three), it means all. Every one of you has the means of opening (the road) to Earthmaker (God). It is given to you. With that (your belief) you can open (the door to God). You can not open it with knowledge (alone). How many letters are there to the key (the road to God)? Three. What are they?" There were many educated people (there), but none of them said anything. "The first (letter) must be a K, so if a person said K, that would be the whole of it. But let me look in the book (the Bible) and see what that means," said the body. Then it (the body) took the Bible and began to turn the leaves. The body did not know where it was itself, for it was not learned in books. Finally in Matthew, chapter 16, it stopped. There it speaks about it. "Peter did not give himself up" (it says). "For a long time he could not give up his own knowledge. There (in that passage) it says Key." That is the work of Earthmaker (God). At least so I understand it. He made use of my body and acted in this manner, in the case of the peyote.

Then I go about telling (every one) that this religion is good. Many other people at home said the same thing. Many, likewise, have joined this religion and are getting along nicely.

On one occasion, after I had eaten a good deal of peyote, I learned the following from it: that all I had done in the past, that it had all been evil. This was plainly revealed to me. What I thought was holy, and (by thus. thinking) was lost, that I now know was false. (It is false), this giving of (pagan) feasts, of holding (the old) things holy, the Medicine Dance, and all the Indian customs.

J.B.'S ACCOUNT OF HIS CONVERSION

I was at the old agency. There they were to try me for murder. At night, as I sat in jail, certain people came to me and told me that they had a gallon jug of whisky, and that if I was free that night, I should come and drink with them. They would wait for me. That same night there was a peyote meeting at John Rave's house and my brother Sam invited me to go there. Sam stood around there waiting for me. He was very low in spirits. He knew of the other invitation I had received and he told me that he would go with me wherever I went. I wanted very badly to go to the place where they had the liquor, and should have done so if Sam had given me the least chance. However, I could not get rid of him, so I decided to go to the peyote meeting. When I arrived there, we found just enough room in the center for myself and Sam. Sam sat at the right of me and John Bear at the left. In front of me there was some peyote infusion, and some peyote ground up and dampened.

As we sat there Sam began to cry and I began to think. I knew why Sam was crying; he wanted me to take some of the peyote. After a while I began to think of my own troubles. But I thought it wasn't the proper way of taking it just because I was in trouble. Then I thought of the other peyote eaters, how much they must be wanting me to take it. After a while I spoke to Sam and said, "I am going to eat this medicine, but . . ." Then I began to cry. After a while he tried to get me to say the balance, but I couldn't. I drank some of the solution. As the others saw that I was willing to take it they gave me a big ball of dampened peyote. However, I didn't like that and I asked for some more peyote in the dry state. I sat there asking for more and more peyote. This I kept up all night. When morning came I stopped. Just then Harry Rave got up to speak, and no sooner did he get up than I knew exactly what he was going to say. This must be the way of all peyote eaters, I thought. I looked around me; and suddenly I realized that all those within the room knew my thoughts and that I knew the thoughts of all the others. Harry Rave spoke and finished his speech; but I had known it all before he said a word. Then A. Priest, who was leading the meeting, arose and asked the rest to get up, so that they might turn themselves over to Christ. I also rose; but when I got up I was seized with a choking sensation. I couldn't breathe. I wanted to grab hold of Bear and Sam, but I didn't, thinking that I was going to stand whatever was coming to me. When I made up my mind to that, I felt relieved. Then I knew what the real meaning of turning one's self over to Christ meant.

In the morning they stopped the meeting and everyone seemed happy and glad. I, however, was very serious and wondered why they were all laughing. Every once in a while they would come and talk to me. I wondered why they did it, when they knew what was going on within me. For that reason I wouldn't answer them.

That week there were four meetings, and I went to all of them and ate very much peyote. The fourth meeting was at the usual place, John Rave's house. I sat with Sam as usual. At night I became filled with peyote. All at once I heard a voice saying, "You are the one who is to tell of the medicine dance." And I thought that Sam was speaking to me, so I turned around and looked at him, but he hadn't said a word. Soon I realized that nobody near me had said anything, and I began to think, "Why should it be I? Why not one of the others?" I rather pushed the idea from me; but no sooner had I done so than I began to have a tired and depressed sensation. This passed all over me. I knew that if I got up with the sincere purpose of giving in to the power that was wanting me to speak of the medicine dance I should be relieved. However, for some reason, I know not why, I felt like resisting.

The next morning I asked to be baptized, and said that I would thereafter have nothing more to do with offerings to the spirits; that I would not give any more feasts; and that I would not have any more to do with the medicine dance. From that day on I quit all my old beliefs. I did not feel like saying all this, for indeed my heart was turned just the other way, but I couldn't help it, for I was filled with the peyote.

From that time on, at every meeting that I attended, I could not rid myself of the idea that I must tell of the medicine dance. At all such times a feeling of heaviness would come over me. There I would be with but one thing on my mind; should I, or should I not, tell of it? I did not want to, and thought of all sorts of excuses—that I was not a member of the Nebraska division, etc.

I was in this frame of mind while living with John Walker. There I received word that I would be wanted to tell of the medicine dance. From that moment I could not rest easy. I went to the barn and prayed and wept, asking that God might direct me. I went about but could not sit quiet. My wife stayed around me crying. As I stood there, someone drove up with a white team. Then I thought of all the unhappiness I would cause to members of the medicine lodge if I told the secrets of the medicine dance; and I asked myself if it really would not be a sin to cause so much misery. The man who was driving the white team was John Baptiste, and he told me that I was wanted to tell of the medicine dance. I got ready and entered the buggy. I was still crying and praying. Then it occurred to me that I would like to see John Rave. No sooner had I thought of this than John Rave appeared in the road. I got out and shook hands with him and told him where I was going and for what purpose, and asked him what he thought of the matter. He began to thank me for the work I was going to do and said, "This is what we should try to do, to help one another and to work for our Creator." Then he thanked me again. Perfect happiness now came over me and I went to Sioux City and got married legally. From now on I was entirely filled with the desire to tell all that I knew about the medicine dance. "This must be the work assigned to me by the Creator," I thought; and yet I have rejected the idea all the time.

On Paul's last trip, although I had not finished the translation, I didn't care to have any more to do with it, and said that somebody else should finish the work, my excuse being that I was busy. So, as soon as I heard that Paul had come, I packed up and hurried out west as quickly as possible, for I knew that he would bother the life out of me if he found me. However, no sooner had I reached the home of my friend than I was seized with an attack of rheumatism, with which I had never been afflicted before, and the next morning Paul appeared with a wagon to take me back to Winnebago. Now I know that the telling and the translation of the medicine dance is my mission in life, and I am willing to tell all to the full extent of my knowledge.

JESSE CLAY'S ACCOUNT OF THE ARAPAHO MANNER OF GIVING THE PEYOTE, CEREMONY WHICH HE INTRODUCED AMONG THE WINNEBAGO IN 1912

I went to Oklahoma once as the guest of an Arapaho Indian. While there I witnessed the Arapaho manner of holding a peyote meeting and was very much impressed with it. A year later this Arapaho came to visit me in Winnebago, and while he was with us a few of my friends urged me to hold the peyote ceremony according to the Arapaho method. I held several meetings at which my Arapaho friend led.

Now these are the instructions that Arapaho Bull gave me.

The person giving the ceremony must get up at sunrise so that he can tell exactly where the sun is going to rise. He must place a stick and make the drawing of a cross on the earth just in that direction from which the sun is about to rise. He does this in order to get the correct location for the tipi and the fireplace. Then he marks a circle around the cross. Then he makes a diagonal mark through the center of the circle, thus making the circle resemble a star. The circle is the outline of the tipi. Then another diagonal mark is made so that the drawing resembles, to their minds, a peyote. A fireplace which resembles a half-moon is placed right in the center of the lodge. After that the tipi poles are raised, 12 in number. Finally the whole is inclosed in canvas. When finished it is supposed to represent the earth. It is then ready to be entered. Special preparations are made for entering. The drummer with his drum and the leader and those behind him with all their regalia march up to the door. Before these enter, however, an attendant, called the fireman, spreads sage all over the lodge, from the seat of the leader to the door and back again. Then he starts a fire, always placing the left fire sticks first. When they are all thus lined up outside of the door the leader offers a prayer.

"May the Creator be with us when we enter this lodge."

The leader now enters and, proceeding along the left side of the lodge, marches to his seat, and there he stands with his drum until the lodge is filled. After all have entered they sit down. Then the fireman who sits to the right rekindles the fire. The leader now spreads out his articles—a gourd, a drumstick, a staff, and the feathers. He then takes 12 sage leaves and lays them out in the form of a star, first making a cross-shaped object and then filling this into the desired form. On top he places the peyote, and, leaning against that, be places a flute made of an eagle bone, the mouth of the flute resting against the peyote. Then he puts an otter-skin cap at the foot of the flute. After a while the leader takes the peyote he is going to use in one hand and some cedar needles in the other, and, going to his seat, where all the other objects are spread out, he sits down and prays. He prays that all the participants may be strengthened by the prospective meeting. He offers up thanks for the peyote and prays that all may be in the proper spirit that night. Then he throws the needles in the fire and holds the peyote over the smoke of the cedar. When this has been finished he returns to his seat, eats one peyote, and gives one to the drummer. After they have eaten these he passes four peyote in turn to those on his left until the peyote comes to the one sitting nearest the door. Four peyote are given to the one nearest the door that he, in turn, may pass them to those on the other side of the door and so on until the leader is reached again. Before the peyote is eaten, the leader gets up and talks.

He instructs the people as to the nature of the meeting and tells them that those who wish to go out must do so after the midnight water is drunk and not until after the leader returns from outside. No one is to go out while anyone is singing, praying, or eating peyote. He then speaks of the special prayers that are to be offered up and asks them to offer general prayers for all nonmembers and even for their enemies. After that the leader again offers up a prayer and smokes all the objects he had spread before his seat. Then the songs are to start, all, however, first eating peyote.

(When the fire first starts and thereafter, throughout the night, it is supposed to represent light, just as God said, "Let there be light.")

The first song is always the same and is called the starting song. Those that follow are peyote songs. When he has finished these songs he passes the singing staff to the right of the drummer. When this one has finished the staff is returned to the leader, who passes it on to the left, and then in rotation it goes to the one sitting near the door. The drum, when it is handed on, is always passed under the staff. The fire is always replenished, but toward midnight special care is taken in this regard and the coals are placed in the shape of a crescent between the fire and the earth crescent, and the fireman sweeps first around the left and then around the right side. Then exactly at midnight the leader calls for his singing staff and his drum, no matter where they happen to be, and, taking the singing staff and sending the drum to the drummer, he blows his flute and sings. The song he sings then is called the midnight song. After that three peyote songs are sung, it making no difference which they are. As the leader starts his midnight song the fireman takes up his position at the doorway opposite the fireplace and the leader. When the second song is started the fireman turns around to the right and goes out and gets water and soon comes back with it. When he reenters he makes the figure of a cross on the ground where he stood just before he left and places water on it. Then he squats down on his knees.

When the leader stops singing he walks to the crescent by the fireplace and begins praying again. After the prayer he burns some more cedar needles. The reason for drinking water at midnight is because Christ was born at midnight and because of the good tidings that he brought to the earth, for water is one of the best things in life and Christ is the savior of mankind. After the leader has made his prayer and the cedar is burned, then the fireman reaches over toward the smoke and makes a motion with his body as if he were drawing the smoke over himself. He then takes the water and brings it over to the leader. The leader takes a bunch of feathers and, dipping it into the water, sprinkles it on the peyote, then on the fire, on the sage, and finally all over the lodge, beginning with the doorway and then going around. The water is then drunk in a regular order, first by the leader, then by the drummer, and then by all the other people. After all these things have been done the leader returns the staff to the man from whom he had taken it at midnight. As soon as this man starts the singing again the leader takes his flute and goes outside. He goes toward the east for a short distance, and there he sits down and offers up a prayer for the people. Then he blows his flute, and going to the south of the lodge repeats the same procedure. This is also repeated for the west and the north. When the singing within the lodge has stopped, he returns and takes his seat.

The purpose of going to the four directions and blowing the flute is to announce the birth of Christ to all the world.

After the leader has reentered the singing continues as before. At daybreak the fireman fixes the fire in the same way as at midnight. The staff, drum, etc., is now passed to the leader, who as soon as he has received everything takes his flute and blows on it. Before doing this, however, he puts on his otter-skin cap. The purpose of blowing the flute just at that time is to represent the trumpet of the Day of Judgment, when Christ will appear wearing His crown in all glory. The putting on of the otter-skin cap represents the crown.

The song used on this occasion is called the water song. After the first song is finished the fireman opens the door and a woman enters carrying water, which she pours over the cross which the fireman had sprinkled at midnight. The fireman then spreads something for her to sit on, between the water and the door.

When the leader has finished his four songs, he lays down his staff, etc., and, taking some cedar needles, offers up a prayer of thanks, and as he finishes he throws the cedar into the fire and sits down while the woman gathers the smoke toward her in the same way as the fireman had done on the previous night. Then the leader takes a drinking cup and sends it toward the woman. The fireman now rises and pours water on the impressions he had made when drawing the cross on the earth, and the woman drinks some water from the cup, which she then returns to the leader. The water is then returned to her and she passes it around the lodge, beginning at the left. When it reaches the leader again, he takes out the same cup which he had handed to the woman and drinks out of it. The water, however, is passed on until it reaches the door. The fireman would then take it and bring it back to where it had been placed when first brought in. The woman rises and goes around the fireplace from left to right, taking the water with her. Finally the leader takes his singing staff and sings four songs. When these songs are finished, the woman places some food just outside the door. The fireman goes outside and brings in this food, placing it in a line between the fire and the door. Four things are brought in—water, corn with sweetened water, fruit, and meat. When the food is brought in the leader puts away all the objects he had spread out before him, which the fireman takes out of the lodge. The leader then offers up a prayer of thanks and says grace. The four kinds of food are passed around the lodge, beginning with the entrance, from left to right. After they are returned they are placed in line again, only in the reverse order from that used before. The fireman then takes them outside. While the people are eating the door remains open.

(During the evening the leader represents the first created man, the woman dressed up is the New Jerusalem, the bride waiting for the bridegroom. The cup used by the leader and the woman is supposed to symbolize the fact that they are to become one; the water represents the God's gift, His Holiness. The corn represents the feast to be partaken of on the Day of Judgment and the fruit represents the fruit of the tree of life. The meat represents the message of Christ and those who accept it will be saved.) [1]

The above descriptions represent the Peyote cult as it was given between 1908 and 1913. It is quite clear that a definite organization exists consisting of a unit of five positions occupied by the leader and four helpers. No specific requirements, with the exception, of course, of that of being a peyote eater, are associated with the right to occupy these positions.

No specialized features have become associated with the positions of the four helpers. As indicated before, John Rave is always the leader when he is present, but the position of leadership can be delegated to others. This is always of a

---

[1] J.C.'s account ends here.

temporary nature. It may be significant to note that whenever delegated the leadership is always delegated to men who have been among the first of the converts, outside of Rave's immediate family, and who were leaders in the old pagan ceremonies. In 1910 this delegation of leadership was clearly a recent tendency, conditioned, on the one hand, by the size of the reservation and the impossibility of Rave's being everywhere, and, on the other hand, by Rave's frequent absence on proselytizing missions. In 1913 it had already become customary for a number of men to hold the position of leader even when Rave was present. A further complication was introduced when Jesse Clay began giving the peyote ceremonies in the Arapaho manner, for he then stood in the same relation to his method of giving the ceremony as Rave stood to the older form. As we shall see, there was, even in 1908, a separatist movement led by Albert Hensley, which, if it had succeeded, would have given Hensley the same leadership that Rave enjoyed before him and that Clay subsequently acquired.

DEVELOPMENT OF THE RITUALISTIC COMPLEX

FROM the accounts given by various members of the Peyote cult it is quite clear that Rave became interested in the peyote on one of his many trips to Oklahoma. According to the verbal account he gave, which differs in some respects from the account he subsequently dictated on the particular visit which resulted in his first eating the peyote, he was in a most distressed and unhappy condition of mind owing to the loss of his wife and children.[1] He went away from Winnebago with the intention of staying away as long as possible from the scene of his loss.

Rave's account of his conversion gives a sufficiently dramatic picture of how he first ate the peyote and its immediate effects. In response to numerous questions as to how he was first induced to eat the peyote he always said that it was because he had been so frequently asked. It is, however, far more likely that he was passing through an emotional crisis at that particular time, and the requests that he partake of it and the inducements held out to him, made it easier for him to succumb then than on his previous visits.

---

[1] In the account Rave himself gives he speaks of seeing his wife and children. As his verbal statement was corroborated by other people, we are inclined to believe that in his dictated account of his conversion he had forgotten the actual state of affairs. It may, of course, be that in his ardent desire to show the marvelous effects of the peyote he permitted his memory to play him false.

To judge from Rave's remarks, his first belief in the peyote had nothing of the nature of a conversion to a new religion. It seems to have been similar to the average Winnebago attitude toward a medicinal plant obtained either as a gift or through purchase. There is only one new note—stimulation by a narcotic.

Rave states that the peyote cured him of a disease with which he had been afflicted for a long time. After repeated requests his wife also consents to being treated; so he paints her face and, taking the rattle, sings peyote songs while she eats the peyote. His attitude throughout, both from his own testimony and from that of others, seems to have been practically the attitude of the Winnebago shaman. He even offered tobacco to the peyote.

We have, then, at the beginning the introduction of apparently only one new element—the peyote, with possibly a few Christian teachings. Everything else seems to be typically Winnebago, and in consonance with their shamanistic practices. On the whole, the extension of the Winnebago cultural background seems to have keen so instantaneous that so far as the specific cultural traits of the Winnebago are concerned there was hardly anything new at all. This view does not, of course, interfere in the least with the fact that to the Winnebago themselves the presence of the peyote represented the introduction of a new element.

The elaboration of the peyote practices at Rave's hands is the most difficult problem to trace on account of the lack of data. In the account that he gives of his conversion there is no evidence whatsoever of any antagonistic attitude toward the old Winnebago manner of living. When the author met him, however, for the first time, in 1908, this passive attitude had changed to one of violent hatred for the old Winnebago customs. Why and under what circumstances this change took place we do not know. It probably represented the interaction of many elements, the hostility of the tribe, the drawing of issues sharply around certain points, and the gradual assumption on the part of Rave of the rôle of a prophet who had solved the problem of the adjustment of the Winnebago to the surrounding white civilization. Offhand, one might be inclined to believe that Rave's insistence upon breaking with the past was due entirely to the influence of the Christian elements incorporated in his new religion. It is, however, extremely doubtful whether such an assumption is necessary. There seem to have been comparatively few Christian elements in the religion before Albert Hensley's influence had made itself felt, yet many of the old war bundles had been destroyed long before that time, and the peyote eaters were looked upon with cordial dislike by the conservative members of the tribe. The admonition that only a complete break with the past could save the Winnebagoes and enable them to compete successfully with the white intruders had been given to the Winnebagoes once before by the famous Shawnee prophet. What the latter claimed, however, was that the various sacred objects used by the Winnebago had lost their power, and that that power must now be renewed. This he thought could only be done by returning to the old manner of living which he claimed the Winnebago were no longer following. Such a claim was, after all, not revolutionary. It is not, therefore, the break with the Winnebago present-day viewpoint that characterizes Rave's attitude, but the fact that instead of returning to the older, purer life as the Shawnee prophet proposed to do, he substituted an alien religion. It was because he was introducing an alien religion, not because he was introducing a new religion, that he was so intensely hated by the conservative members of the tribe.

When this hostility was at its height a new convert, Albert Hensley, revolutionized the entire cult by introducing the reading of the Bible, postulating the dogma that the peyote opened the Bible to the understanding of the people, and also adding a number of Christian practices. He, like Rave, had been in Oklahoma. He brought back with him many peyote songs, generally in other languages, dealing with Christian ideas, upon which subsequently Winnebago songs were modeled. He also introduced either baptism itself or an interpretation of baptism, and induced Rave to attempt a union with the Christian Church. He seems to have been the only prominent man connected with the peyote who was subject to epileptic fits. He had the most glorious visions of heaven and hell while in his trance, and these he expounded afterwards in terms of Revelation and the mystical portions of the New Testament. Hensley's additions represent a second stratum of borrowed elements, all of which are in the nature of accretions as far as the peyote itself is concerned. The Bible is explained in terms of the peyote. Neither Hensley nor his followers ever interpreted the peyote in terms of the Bible, although other elements of the old Winnebago culture were so interpreted. These elements, however, represented features that even in the old Winnebago cults exhibited a great variability in interpretation.

Rave's attitude toward the innovations of Hensley seems to have been that of a benevolent acquiescence. He himself could neither read nor write. Yet he immediately accepted the Bible and added it to his other regalia. As such it always seems to have remained. To Rave, after all, the peyote was the principal element, and if Hensley chose to insist that the Bible was only intelligible to those who partook of the peyote why that naturally fell within its magical powers. From the entire omission in Rave's account of the Peyote cult of the more important things that Hensley introduced and from the fact that whenever Hensley's influence was not dominant there seems to have been little Bible reading, it seems justifiable to say that Rave's attitude toward these innovations was merely passive.

There never was any rivalry between Rave and Hensley. The latter was, however, a much younger man, quick-tempered, conceited, dogmatic, and withal having a strong mixture of Puritan Protestant ideas. A conflict developed after a while and in a very interesting manner. Rave had allowed a man with an extremely bad reputation, who had been admitted as a member of the Peyote cult, to occupy one of the four positions. Hensley violently protested, on the ground that a man of X.'s character could not properly perform the rites associated with that position. Rave, however, retorted that the efficacy of the peyote, of any position connected with its cult, was in no way connected with the character of the performer, and that it was inherent in the peyote and in the Peyote ritual. Thereupon, after much parleying to and fro, Hensley formally seceded, taking with him a number of followers. The bulk of the peyote eaters, however, remained with Rave, and within a comparatively short time a number of Hensley's followers returned to Rave, so that in 1911 Hensley had merely a handful of people. Since then he has ceased to be a force, although his innovations have been retained by a number of the younger Peyote members, especially by those who read English.

In 1911 there was no unification of the ideas of Rave and Hensley. Since then, strange to say, although Hensley's attempt to set up his own religion failed utterly, his ideas and Christian innovations seemed to have triumphed completely. This, however, has gone hand in hand with a marked dropping off of enthusiasm. It appears now as if the Peyote cult has run its course. Some of the members have recently returned— to the old pagan customs, others have practically become Christians, and many have become indifferent.

Unquestionably the most interesting of recent innovations is that introduced by Jesse Clay, the account of which has been given before. This is, of course, the Arapaho manner of conducting the ceremony. At the present time it has none of the characteristics of the Winnebago ceremonial. Whether in the next few years it will develop any depends upon the interest manifested in it by the Peyote worshipers and upon the vitality of the Peyote movement in general.

It is extremely suggestive to compare what Rave introduced with the ceremony borrowed by Clay. The former introduced an isolated element, the peyote and its worship, and clothed it almost immediately in characteristic Winnebago forms. It can truly be said that although the peyote is an alien element, from the Winnebago viewpoint, everything else in the ceremony is and was from the beginning typically Winnebago. Clay's method of conducting the Peyote ceremonies, on the other hand, is entirely alien. For it ever to become popular with the large mass of Winnebago it will have to become thoroughly assimilated with the Winnebago background.

DISSEMINATION OF THE DOCTRINE

LET us now see how the ideas of Rave and Hensley were transmitted in the tribe itself, who the first and the later converts were, in what the nature of their conversion consisted, and what they, in turn, brought to the new cult.

The first and foremost virtue predicated by Rave for the peyote was its curative power. He gives a number of instances in which hopeless venereal diseases and consumption were cured by its use; and this was the first thing one heard about it as late as 1913. In the early days of the Peyote cult it appears that. Rave relied principally for new converts upon the knowledge of this great curative virtue of the peyote. The main point apparently was to induce people to try it. No amount of preaching of its direct effects, such as the hyperstimulation induced, the glorious visions, and the feeling of relaxation following, would ever have induced prominent members of the old Winnebago religious societies to try it. For that reason it is highly significant that all the old members of the Peyote cult speak of the diseases of which it cured them. Along this line lay unquestionably its appeal for the most converts. Its subsequent spread was due to a large number of interacting factors. One informant claims that there was little religion connected with it at first, and that the people drank the peyote on account of its peculiar effects.

The manner in which it spread at the beginning was simple and significant—viz, along family lines. As soon as an individual had become a peyote eater he devoted all his energies to converting other members of his family. From instances that have come to our notice this lay in an insistent appeal to family ties and personal affection. A man showed unusual courtesy, showered innumerable favors upon relatives he was anxious to convert, and thereby earned the gratitude of the recipient, who at some critical moment, let us say, such as illness or mental depression, showed it by partaking of the peyote. The same methods were employed in the more general propaganda. The author knows of Peyote people who drove many miles in order to be present at the bedside of some old conservative who was ill, perhaps neglected by his relatives; bring him food, and spend the night with him in the most affectionate solicitude. They always had sufficient tact and understanding of human nature not to obtrude their purpose on the sick man too much. To the casual observer their object seemed simply that of a Samaritan. They would hardly have admitted that behind all their solicitude lay the desire to obtain a new convert. They would have claimed that their only purpose, over and above their sincere desire to comfort the sick man, was to demonstrate to their fellow Winnebago what changes the peyote had wrought in them. In this way the patient drew the inference, an inference that was likely to be drawn all the more quickly and forcibly when he contrasted the behavior of these Peyote nurses with that of his pagan relatives. The author was fortunate enough to obtain a fairly complete account of a conversion, illustrating both these features.

WHAT THE CONVERTS INTRODUCED

IT is quite impossible to establish now what these converts introduced individually. For that matter it is not necessary to assume that they brought any specific additions to the cult. What they did bring were Winnebago; and with that, the emotional and cultural setting of the old pagan background. To one, the eating of the peyote gave the same magical powers that were formerly associated with membership in the medicine dance; to another, the visions were direct blessings from God, directing him to perform certain actions; to a third, faithfulness to the teachings of the Peyote cult became associated with a certainty of reaching God, of being able to take the right road in the journey to the spirit land. Even a man so thoroughly saturated with Christian doctrines as Hensley himself felt it necessary to introduce an origin myth; and although we know that he borrowed it from a southern tribe, it is quite clear that in Hensley's narrative it has already assumed all the characteristics of a Winnebago fasting experience and ritualistic myth, similar to those connected with the founders of the old Winnebago cult societies. In its totality the atmosphere of the Peyote cult became thus charged with the old Winnebago background. In 1911 it can not be said that they had displaced the distinctive Christian elements. Among the younger members, especially those who had been trained in the east and could read and write English, the influence of the Christian ideas in the interpretation of the old pagan features is, as was pointed out before, so strong to-day that it threatens to displace the others.

The following homily will show how the old myths were used by the younger Peyote members to point a tale.

The old people often spoke of the Trickster, but we never knew what they meant. They told us how he wrapped a coon-skin blanket around himself and went to a place where all the people were dancing. There he danced until evening and then he stopped and turned around. No one was to be seen anywhere, and then he realized that he had mistaken for people dancing the noise made by the wind blowing through the reeds.

So do we Winnebagoes act. We dance and make a lot of noise, but in the end, we accomplish nothing.

Once, as the Trickster was going toward a creek, he saw a man standing on the other side, dressed in a black suit, and pointing his finger at him. He spoke to the man but the latter would not answer. Then he spoke again and again, but without receiving any reply. Finally he got angry and said, "See here! I can do that too." He put on the black coat and pointed his finger across the creek. Thus both of them stood all day. Toward evening, when he looked around again, he noticed that the man across the creek, pointing his finger at him, was really just a tree stump. "O my! what have I been doing all this time? Why did I not look before I began? No wonder the people call me the Foolish One."

So are we Winnebagoes. We never look before we act. We do everything without thinking. We think we know all about it.

The Trickster was walking around with a pack on his back. As he walked along, someone called to him. "Say, we want you to sing." "All right," said he. "I am carrying songs in my pack, and if you wish to dance, build a large lodge for me with a small hole at the end for an entrance." When it was finished, they all went in, and the Trickster followed them. Those who had spoken to him were birds. He told them that while dancing they were not to open their eyes, for if they did their eyes would become red. Whenever a fat bird passed the Trickster he would choke it to death, and if it cried out, he would say, "That's it! That's it! Give a whoop!"

After a while one of the birds got somewhat suspicious and opened its eyes just the least little bit. He saw that the Trickster was choking all the birds. "He is killing us all," said the bird. "Let all who can run for their lives." Then he flew out through the top of the house. The Trickster took the birds he had killed and roasted them; but he did not get a chance to eat. them, for they were taken away from him by somebody.

So are we Winnebagoes. We like all that is forbidden. We say that we like the medicine dance; we say that it is good and yet we keep it secret and forbid people to witness it. We tell members of the dance not to speak about it until the world shall come to an end. They are afraid to speak of it. We, the Winnebago, are the birds, and the Trickster is satan.

Once, as the Trickster was going along the road, some one spoke to him. He listened, and he heard it say, "If anyone eats me all bad things will come out of him." Then the trickster went up to the one talking, and said, "What is your name?" "My name is 'Blows-himself-away.'" The Trickster would not believe it; so he ate it. After a while, he blew himself away. He laughed. "Oh, pshaw! I suppose this is what it meant." As he went along it grew worse and worse, and it was only after the greatest hardship that he succeeded in returning home.

So are we Winnebagoes. We travel on this earth all our lives, and then when one of us tastes something that makes him unconscious we look upon this thing with suspicion when he regains consciousness.

THE ATTITUDE OF THE CONSERVATIVES

AT every phase of the cult's development Rave had to contend with the hostility of the conservative members of the tribe. It would be interesting to know in what manner and degree this hostility manifested itself upon the first introduction of the peyote. As we have seen, there was in the beginning little difference between the beliefs relating to the peyote and those connected with the old Winnebago medicinal plants. Nevertheless the author was assured that hostility was exhibited to the new cult from the very start. Would the same hostility have been exhibited had this new feature represented some development from within the tribe? In other words, what it would be interesting to know, is whether the fact that the peyote was derived from without led to a hostility different in kind from that exhibited toward an innovation developing within the culture itself. No evidence could be obtained that would justify us in explaining the hostility felt by the older conservative Winnebago as due in any part to the fact that it was alien in origin. Certain elements that to-day form an integral part of the most popular of all Winnebago ceremonies were borrowed from the Sauk and Iowa, and the Winnebago realize this and mention it in the introductory myths told in connection with the preparatory rites of the medicine dance. The explanation obtained was always the same—that the hostility was due to the fact that the teachings of the Peyote people departed from those of their ancestors and that the Peyote were simply aping the habits and customs of the whites. What seems to have met with the greatest opposition from the older shamans was the denial of the doctrine of reincarnation. The Christian doctrine of the immortality of the soul does not seem to have been felt as a substitute at all. One old conservative assured the author that he had long ago prophesied the appearance of the peyote among the Winnebago. He told the author the following:

"This medicine is one of the four spirits from below, and for that reason it is a bad thing. These spirits have always longed for human beings and now they are getting hold of them. Those who use this medicine claim that when they die they will only be going on a long journey. But that is not the truth, for when they eat peyote they destroy their spirits, and death to them will mean extermination. If I spit upon the floor, the sputum will soon dry up and nothing will remain of it. So death will be for them. I might go out and preach against this doctrine, but it would be of no avail, for I certainly would not be able to draw more than one or two people away from this spirit. Many will be taken in by this medicine; they will not be able to help themselves in any way. The bad spirit will certainly seize them."

www.ingramcontent.com/pod-product-compliance
Lightning Source LLC
Chambersburg PA
CBHW061224070526
44584CB00029B/3978